hAIku

volume I

personal responsibility from A to Z

Dedicated to my wife and kids.

Thanks for being my biggest supporters.

hAIku

volume I
personal responsibility from A to Z

prompted by
David Pengelley

text generated by
OpenAI chatGPT-3

images generated by
Canva **® Text-to-Image**

hAIku: Volume 1 - Personal Responsibility from A to Z
Copyright © 2023 Valid Agenda Pty Ltd

Formatting & Editing by David Pengelley

ISBN 978-0-6458217-0-3 (Paperback)
SBN 978-0-6458217-1-0 (Hardcover)

Enquiries may be directed to publishing@validagenda.com

AI Prompt - Artificial Intelligence enhancing human potential

FOREWARD (WRITTEN BY HUMAN)

Artificial Intelligence (AI) is evolving rapidly and at the same time so many humans would observably appear to be devolving.

What do I mean by humans are devolving? We live in an era when there is so much abundance and prosperity (or at least the potential for such). This abundance is the accomplishment of many men and women's hard work, perseverance and ingenuity which should not be taken for granted. However, the relative ease of modern life, the accessibility of food, power and pleasure has bred a discontent and for some even a contempt and disdain for those who came before, and most often by those who have given little and accomplished nothing themselves.

This sense of entitlement often manifests in a perceived victimhood. These victims when encountering any problems or impediments to their immediate gratification perceive it as a personal attack. Reparations are then demanded from someone who would appear to have more (be it money, status, influence etc.) regardless of the objective truth, the victim never owns the blame, it's always somebody else's fault.

AI remains to be seen if it will be wielded for good or evil (and most likely a good measure of both), but while the jury is out I set to the task of having it generate an A-Z of haiku to promote the concept and benefits of personal responsibility. If a computer is able to comprehend and concisely capture what it means and why it matters to have some personal agency and take personal responsibility, maybe, just maybe there is hope for us humans after all.

- David Pengelley

HOW WAS AI LEVERAGED TO WRITE THIS BOOK?

100% of Haiku content was generated by the free preview version of OpenAI's chatGPT-3. It took a few iterations to get the desired A-Z output but the core of the initial prompt was simply "Write a table of haikus about personal responsibility".

Each entire haiku was entered into Canva's text to image generator to create the corresponding image found on each page.

ALWAYS CHOOSE TO ACT,

ACCOUNTABLE FOR
OUR DEEDS,

ACCEPTING THE TRUTH

BELIEVE IN ONESELF,

BEACON OF HOPE
AND COURAGE,

BRAVERY TO SHINE

CONSCIOUSNESS WITHIN,

CONTEMPLATING LIFE'S
GREAT DEEDS,

CONNECTING WITH ALL

DUTY TO ONESELF,

DETERMINATION TO ACT,

DIRECTION IN LIFE

EVERY ACTION COUNTS,

EMPOWERMENT TO
CHOOSE RIGHT,

ETHICS GUIDE US ALL

FORGIVENESS IS KEY,

FACING UP TO
PAST MISTAKES,

FREEDOM TO MOVE ON

GIVING OUR BEST SELVES,

GRATITUDE FOR
WHAT WE HAVE,

GENEROSITY GROWS

HONESTY IS STRENGTH,

HONOR IN WORD
AND IN DEED,

HOLDING OURSELVES TRUE

INTENTION TO SERVE,

INSPIRATION TO GIVE MORE,

IMPACT ON THE WORLD

Joy in the journey,

Judgment made with a
clear mind,

Justice for all deeds

KINDNESS STARTS WITH US,

KNOWLEDGE GUIDES US
THROUGH LIFE'S MAZE,

KEEP HEART AND STAY TRUE

LOVE FOR ALL BEINGS,

LIVING WITH COMPASSION'S
FIRE,

LEGACY OF LIGHT

MINDFULNESS IN ALL,

MAKING EACH MOMENT
MATTER,

MASTERING ONESELF

NURTURE WHAT IS TRUE,

NOBLE IN THOUGHT AND
ACTION,

NOURISHING THE SOUL

OPENNESS OF HEART,

OWNING UP TO WHAT WE DO,

OVERCOMING FLAWS

PURPOSE GIVES US STRENGTH,

PASSION FUELS OUR
INNER FLAME,

PATHWAY TO SUCCESS

QUEST FOR EXCELLENCE,

QUIETLY SEEKING TO LEARN,

QUESTIONING ALL THINGS

RESPONSIBILITY,

REFLECTING ON OUR ACTIONS,

RESPECTING ALL LIFE

SIMPLICITY WINS,

SAVORING LIFE'S
SIMPLE JOYS,

SERENITY REIGNS

TRUTH IN ALL WE DO,

TAKING OWNERSHIP OF LIFE,

TRIUMPH IN THE END

Unwavering strength,

Understanding our limits,

Unleashing our best

Virtues guide our way,

Values define who we are,

Victory is ours

WISDOM TO DISCERN,

WILL TO ACT UPON WHAT'S
RIGHT,

WORTHWHILE LEGACY

XENIAL IN OUR WAYS,

XENODOCHIALITY,

XENIALITY PAYS

YEARNING TO IMPROVE,

YIELD TO HIGHER
ASPIRATIONS,

YOU ARE THE DRIVER

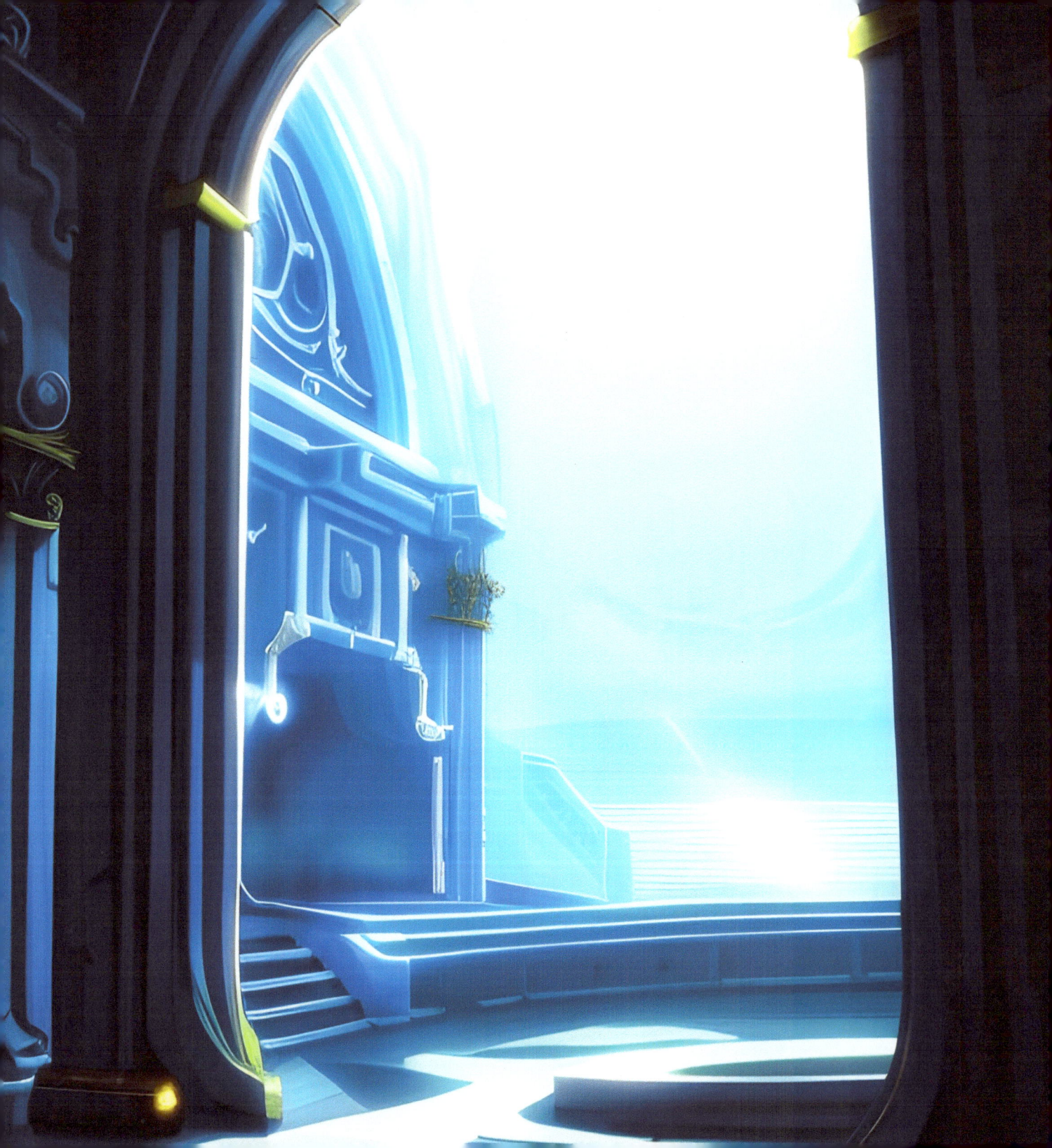

ZEAL TO MAKE A CHANGE,

ZERO TOLERANCE
FOR WRONG DEEDS,

ZENITH IN YOUR GRASP

Appendix
(just the haiku)

A
Always choose to act,
Accountable for our deeds,
Accepting the truth.

B
Believe in oneself,
Beacon of hope and courage,
Bravery to shine.

C
Consciousness within,
Contemplating life's great deeds,
Connecting with all.

D
Duty to oneself,
Determination to act,
Direction in life.

E
Every action counts,
Empowerment to choose right,
Ethics guide us all.

F
Forgiveness is key,
Facing up to past mistakes,
Freedom to move on.

G
Giving our best selves,
Gratitude for what we have,
Generosity grows.

H
Honesty is strength,
Honor in word and in deed,
Holding ourselves true.

I

Intention to serve,
Inspiration to give more,
Impact on the world.

M

Mindfulness in all,
Making each moment matter,
Mastering oneself.

J

Joy in the journey,
Judgment made with a clear mind,
Justice for all deeds.

N

Nurture what is true,
Noble in thought and action,
Nourishing the soul.

K

Kindness starts with us,
Knowledge guides us through life's
maze,
Keep heart and stay true.

O

Openness of heart,
Owning up to what we do,
Overcoming flaws.

L

Love for all beings,
Living with compassion's fire,
Legacy of light.

P

Purpose gives us strength,
Passion fuels our inner flame,
Pathway to success.

Q

Quest for excellence,
Quietly seeking to learn,
Questioning all things.

U

Unwavering strength,
Understanding our limits,
Unleashing our best.

R

Responsibility,
Reflecting on our actions,
Respecting all life.

V

Virtues guide our way,
Values define who we are,
Victory is ours.

S

Simplicity wins,
Savoring life's simple joys,
Serenity reigns.

W

Wisdom to discern,
Will to act upon what's right,
Worthwhile legacy.

T

Truth in all we do,
Taking ownership of life,
Triumph in the end.

X

Xenial in our ways,
Xenodochiality,
Xeniality pays.

Y

Yearning to improve,
Yield to higher aspirations,
You are the driver.

Z

Zeal to make a change,
Zero tolerance for wrong deeds,
Zenith in your grasp.

Unused AI Generated Art

(but I still thought it was cool)

TOLNE

About the Author

David Pengelley is a technology and business strategist with an MBA who builds practical tools for progress. After years leading cross-functional teams, he's been leveraging AI tools and sharing thoughts on how to Keep Moving Forward.

Keep Moving Forward is not about theory. It is about resilience in the face of adversity, sharing insights on adaptability, integrity, and progress – with the goal of helping others build strength and move forward with confidence.

For more tips follow
Dave on his Substack
'Keep Moving Forward'

Other books from David Pengelley

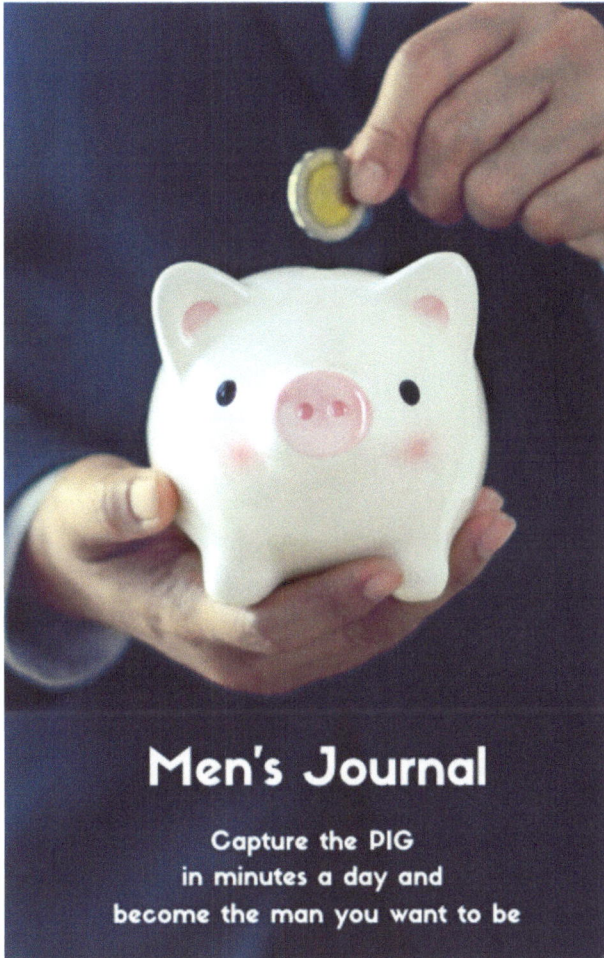

Men's Journal

Capture the PIG
in minutes a day and
become the man you want to be

This is a journal for people who don't journal but want a simple way of getting started. We've all heard it's good for us, but that doesn't make it easy to get started.

Each day you simply take a few minutes to *"catch the **PIG**"*.

How do you capture the PIG? You write down something each day that

- Made you feel **P**roud
- You **I**mproved upon
- You were **G**rateful for

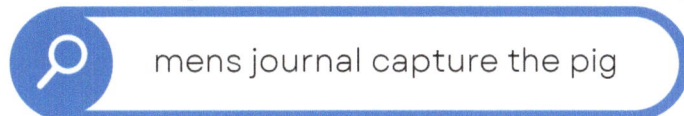